THE VALUES OF THE TWO ANTHEMS AND THE PLEDGE TO NIGERIA

Comparative Studies Of The New And The Old National Anthems With The Pledge In Relation To The Nigerian Value System

Dipo Toby Alakija

ISBN: 978-978-362-401-6
ISBN:978-362-401-6

Printed in United States

Published by

CALVARY ROCK PUBLISHING

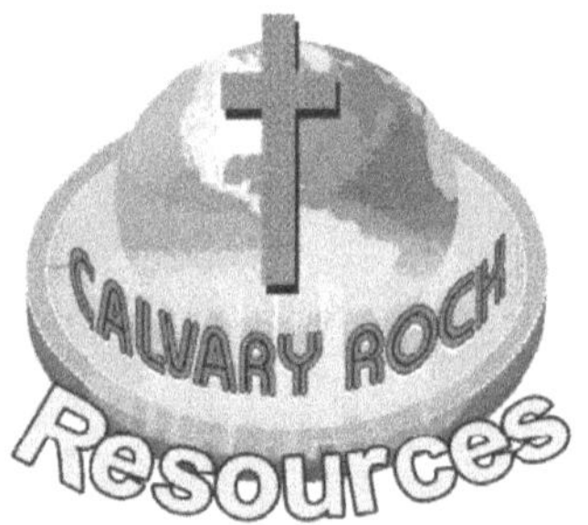

19, Ajina Street, Ikenne Remo,
Ogun State,
Nigeria.

In Conjunction With
CHRISTIAN EDUCATION AND MINISTRATION SERVICES (CEMS)

Dedication

This book is dedicated to all Nigerian parents who are doing all they can to groom their children into reasonable and responsible citizens of Nigeria either within and outside the country.

INTRODUCTION OF NIGERIAN VALUE SYSTEM WITH STORY OF GENERATIONAL SHIP

There is a ship that contains 1st, 2nd and 3rd Generations called Nigeria. The ship is big enough to accommodate more generations that are not yet born.

The 1st Generation made many terrible mistakes but the most catastrophic among them was the failure to teach the 2nd and even 3rd Generations how to preserve the ship, including servicing of all the engines.

The National Value System which is the engine that actually powers others like the economic, political social and other machineries is partly made with the National Anthem and The Pledge To Nigeria. These mistakes resulted into several leakages, causing many damages in virtually all the engines of the ship. Of course, it becomes very difficult if not impossible for the ship to move forward on the sea.

By the time the people in the 1st Generation realized their mistakes, they were too old and weak to rectify the errors. So they counted on the 2nd Generation to do something about the problems that are getting worse everyday. But then, the psyches of most of the people in every Generation is so affected by these problems that very few people are willing to pay the price of providing solutions. In fact, a lot of them benefitted from nearly all the bad systems.

The problems continue to mount up because nothing meaningful is done to solve them until it is no longer safe to stay on the ship. Since the people have no other ship that will take them to their destinations in life, it becomes the civic responsibilities and moral obligations of every generations, including the young ones to begin to find solutions to these problems. Failure to do this will cause the ship to go down and if it goes down, every generation is going down with it.

To provide solutions to these numerous problems and challenges like political issues, social vices, insecurities and crimes like hooliganism; cultism and terrorism in Nigeria, there is need to fix the Nigerian Value System which has other components like Moral, Family, Traditional and Religious Values.

Since the greatest mistake of the people in 1st Generation is their failures to hand over to the 2nd one these core values, all Generations need to learn from it and do everything they can to fix the problems.

NIGERIAN VALUE SYSTEM

Close studies and juxtapositions of the reinstated National Anthem, the new that is now old one and The Pledge To Nigeria reveal the fame work of the National Value System. This frame work which is expected to be built upon by everybody in the positions of leaders, teachers and parents are neglected. The neglect of this frame work is what brings about chaos, vices and crimes in our organized society.

Based on some findings, it is save to conclude that the problems of Nigeria are Nigerians, especially those who have eroded the frame work of the National Value System. To rebuild this frame work, the values of the two National Anthems and The Pledge To Nigeria, which are going to be studied critically need to be appreciated and understood as part of the law

THE NEW NATION ANTHEM OF NIGERIA

The Nation Anthem which is reinstated as the new one was used from independence day in 1960 until in 1978. It was changed in 2024 to the one that is now old.

Students During Independence Day On October 1st 1960

The lyrics of the new Anthem was composed by Lillian Jean Willians, a British expatriate. The melody was composed by Frances Berda and adopted in October 1, 1960.

The new national anthem goes this way:

Nigeria we hail thee,
Our own dear native land,
Though tribe and tongue may differ
In brotherhood we stand,
Nigerians all, and proud to serve
Our sovereign mother land.

Our flag shall be a symbol
That truth and justice reign,
In peace or battle honour'd,
And this we count as gain
To hand on to our children.
A banner without stain

Oh God of all creations
Grant this our one request
Help us to build a nation
Where no man is oppressed,
And so with peace and plenty
Nigeria maybe blessed

Going by the analysis of the reinstated National Anthem, Lillian seemed to have studied the diversities of Nigerian cultures, norms, traditional, family and even religious values properly. She was able to weave them into a National Anthem that appears to project the core Nigerian Values.

ANALYSIS OF THE NEW NATIONAL ANTHEM

Nigeria We Hail Thee: This sounds like a poetic or literary way of giving praise to or an act of calling the attention of someone who is very special and honourable. Nigerians, just like other countries that exist today, are those who make existence of the nation of Nigeria possible. This is later recognized in the descriptions of the tribes and tongues that differ. In other words, Nigerians are made to see themselves as special people, irrespective of their differences. This is vital to note before they can be proud of whom they are.

Our Own Dear Native Land: This is the recognition of all the areas in the Eastern, Western, Southern and Northern parts of the nation as the native land of all Nigerians as it reflects in the constitution. Thus they have the rights to live in any part of the country without feeling like strangers.

Though Tribe And Tongue May Differ, In Brotherhood We Stand: This is description of the fact that though there are different tribes and languages in the native land of all Nigerians but they are made to see themselves as brothers simply because they are of the same citizenship and purposes. Thus they have to stand together as brothers without dwelling on the differences in their tribes and languages.

Nigerians All, And Proud To Serve Our Sovereign Motherland: You will note the use of motherland, which is different from the old anthem that describes Nigeria as "fatherland" but what is common to both is the service to the nation. The aspect of service to Nigeria will be explained later.

Our Flag Shall Be A Symbol: The design of the national flag by Michael Taiwo Akinkunmi (born on 10th May 1936) depicts who Nigerians and what the nation is expected to be.

Pa Michael Taiwo Akinkunmi Who Designed The Flag Of Nigeria

The national flag was designed in 1959 and was officially adopted on the independence day in October 1st 1960. The green, white and green colour symbolize two different things. The white stripe symbolizes peace and unity in the country as it reflects in the two anthems and the pledge to Nigeria while the green symbolizes fertile land, which is one of, if not the major sources of the country's wealth. Although the new national anthem may not explicitly indicate all the symbols in the flag but the next lines indicate peace that may be brought about by truth and justice. Thus the flag, according to this line, symbolizes that the united and peaceful Nigerians dwell in their fertile mother or fatherland.

Nigerian School Children During One Of The Recent Independent Day Celebrations, Holding Nigerian Flag.

That Truth And Justice Reign: Through this line and that of the old anthem, truth and justice are meant to characterize everything about Nigeria for the following reasons:

(i) Without truth, there would be miscarriage of justice.

(ii) Without truth, criminals will appear innocent while innocent people may look like criminals.

(iii) Without truth, leaders would deceive the followers.

(iv) Without truth, especially about the state of the nation either economically or politically or in other things, the country cannot move forward at all.

(v) Without truth, leaders and citizens will be misinformed, making the country to be deformed.

Nigerian Soldiers Go Into Battle With Boko Haram Below

<u>In Peace Or battle Honoured</u>: This line further emphasizes the need for truth and justice to reign. This line indicates that a battle may need to be fought with honour before there can be peace. Or in order to maintain peace, there may be battle to be fought with honour. This battle may not necessarily mean war but struggle to preserve lives and properties or tussles with leaders that abuse their positions, war against political oppressions or economic depressions. Unknown to many Nigerians, lack of truth like declaration of assets of politicians before assuming offices or manipulations of electoral results are injustices that can create rooms for crimes and vices. If Nigerians are made conscious of the need for truth and justice; educating them about their rights, they would be better equipped to wage war against crimes and vices instead of getting involved in any of them.

<u>And These We Count As Gain</u>: The peace and the honour that may be achieved in battle as a result of the prevail of truth and justice in the nation are counted as gain. This line emphasizes the fact that other gains, including financial benefits will soon vanish if peace and honour are not achieved. The reason is that crimes and vices which are threats to lives and properties are expensive to fight. If, however, the truth about a citizen or a situation is discovered, justice must be done to safeguard the interests of the nation.

To illustrate this, I would like to quote from one of my papers that compares the nation as human body with many parts (citizens.) If the body is infected with deadly bacteria (crimes and vices) that threaten the entire system, antidotes (truth and justice) must be applied to save the whole body (the system) from breaking down or getting destroyed. In other words, natural resources or things that bring wealth are not the real wealth of a nation. Real wealth is the peace and honour that reign in the nation. Since the citizens are the ones that bring about peace, they must be made to live in peace by abiding by the law. Justice enforces the law and order in the society. The essence of locking up criminals in prison is not just to punish them but to serve as deterrent to others. In a situation where a criminal is allowed to go away with the crime he has committed, the peace of the nation would be under threat because others maybe encouraged to commit crimes. The government would be forced to spend the gain in the natural and other resources so as to secure lives and properties. For this reason, the real gain is not the financial benefit but the peace and the honour that are achieved while applying truth and justice.

To Hand On Our Children: This line recognizes the fact that children are the future of every nation. The followings prove this to be so:

(i) Children will grow into adults who would later become parents or grand or great parent as years roll by.

(ii) Whatever children of today learn are what will design their lives years later. For this reason, they are and must be compelled by parents or Governments to go to school and learn to be useful and productive in future. Otherwise, they will constitute nuisances like street beggars and even criminals.

(iii) If children learn wrong thing now, it will become very difficult if not impossible to change when they grow up with it. According to the results of series of research works of

A Civil Unrest Scene That Led To Deaths Of Many People In Nigeria.

the author and that of others that are compiled in his book titled "The Insanity Of Humanity," most children who are raised and taught through network of televisions are intellectually dead in their early teens.

The line also implies the legacies that are to be handed over to children, which they will also hand over to their own children. If at any point, bad legacies are handed over to them, they will also hand the same to their children with the bad effect on the nation. Good and bad legacies can be compared with sheep and pigs. If there are ten good legacies which are represented as sheep and two bad legacies which can be considered as pigs, the good legacies can be eroded within a short time if the citizens are not patriotic enough to curb the excesses of bad legacies. This is because bad legacies have different ways of multiplying themselves just like pigs can easily produce themselves in large numbers.

A Banner Without Stain: This line talks about the good legacies which are to be handed over to the children. A lot of legacies (banners) that are stained (bad) had been given to the present generation which is taking their tolls on the nation. These legacies include though not limited to:

(I) Religious Sentiments: Religion is good only when it promotes peace or adds moral value to the people or enhance the National Value System. However, any religion that is enforced either by coercion or manipulation is a violation of fundamental human right as guarantied by the constitution and the gift of freewill that is given by God. The end result is rebellion that may lead to the breakdown of law and order, which is enough to threaten the peace of the nation. Because Nigeria is a secular state, religion can only be offered and accepted or rejected by reasons and logics as perceived by the person to receive it. If it is offered and accepted through this way, this can bring respect to principles of the religion. Thus any religion that encourages violence or bloodshed is a crime. When people become sentimental about a religion to the extent of breaking the law, the children would be offered

bad legacy. They are forced to either join the religious oppressors or fight against them. In either case, the end result is violence.

(ii) Fraudulent Practice: This is a dirty or terrible legacy that is common in every section within the system of Nigeria, ranging from politics; civil service; economic; social and academic to religious and other institutions and organizations or establishments.

The attitudes of most Nigerians, especially youths and some leaders are described as bacteria in the body system (national value system). The bacteria indicate their existence in the body (the society) through rampant vices and crimes. The end result of all these is either the governments spend the fortune of the nation fighting crimes and building more prisons that will accommodate more criminals, doing all they can to secure lives and properties or to rebuild the nation through young ones who are going to be parents and leaders of tomorrow. None of these is an easy may out but the most effective method is to combine the two. In essence, it is deadly to hand over stained (bad) banner (legacy) to young ones.

(iii) Antisocial Behaviours: This is also a stain in the banner (destructive legacy). Nigerians are good at giving good and sound speeches but most do not follow what they say. Many politicians make lofty promises that influence the people to vote for them but when they get into the office, they care only for themselves. Parents at times teach their children good conduct but they themselves misbehave in their presence, making them confused. Teachers teach their students the right thing but they do the wrong thing. Vast majority of Nigerians do not care about saying or doing the right thing at all. Some artists in the bid to be recognized in the society and to make money produce music and movies that corrupt the society, making antisocial behaviour seems like a normal way of life. Most people, including some political and religious leaders do not take cognizance of the fact that antisocial behaviours, which at times begin from homes and schools always spread across the nation through means of entertainment, information, communication and even education. Safeguarding channels of evils at every level in the society is getting much more difficult, if not impossible because of the defective

National Psyche as can be noted in the story about generational ship.

Oh God Of All Creation: This is the first line of the third stanza of the New National Anthem. If this is compared with the first line of the second stanza of the Old Anthem, it would be noted that it is made official that Nigeria as a nation believes in God right from the onset. This is because faith in God plays vital roles in the lifestyles of the people, shaping the National Psyche in a very positive way. Thus faith in God of all creations and praying to Him about the nation as can be noted in this third stanza of the National Anthem are parts of Nigerian civic responsibilities and moral obligations.

Going by results of various research works, the following reasons make it necessary for people to believe there is God:

(I) Without belief in God, a Godless society can be created. Because God is perceive as the Creator of all things including mankind, he has the power to also kill or to destroy or to do whatever He likes to evil people. When people are conscious of this, it makes them feel accountable before God even after they die. If this consciousness of accountability before God is removed from people, they can become dangerous unless the law is forceful enough to make them behave right. Even then, because the law does not have the enforcement agents in every nook and cranny of the society, the people can still commit crimes and get away with them. But with consciousness that God who has all powers is everywhere; seeing everything and having all information, the citizens tend to behave right. So faith in God which the two anthems introduced is not intended to make the people so fanatical to the extent of killing others in the name of any religion but to make them aware that there is God who created everyone, watching everything everybody does either in secret or in the open.

(ii) The belief in God can boost people's moral values. Vladimir Lenin, a Russian dictator who can be considered as the of cause of the deaths of millions of his people said, "there are no moral in politics; there is only experience. A scoundrel may be used to us just because he is a scoundrel." He also added, "Give me four years to teach the children and the seed I have sown will never be uprooted." And he also indicated that the best revolutionists are youths devoid of morals. When you consider his method of ruling Russia you will observe that he first removed every form of belief in God that always boost the people's moral values. When the youths who are always full of energy, going by his theory and activities, were devoid of morals, he would train and use them to eliminate anyone that tried to oppose him or his policies. This method is similar to most other dictators' all over the world. The belief in God thus plays vital role in formation of good conduct and positive attitudes of citizens. Any religion that cannot achieve this is not to be encouraged in anyway.

(iii) The belief in God makes a person committed to one another as a members of the society or mother land.

Grant This Our One Request: The belief in God assures the people that if they pray to him, he will answer them. If their request is granted, it increases their faith in God. If not, it would be assumed that their faith is not strong enough. In whichever way it goes, people; especially young ones are to be taught about the need to talk to God in prayer. The followings are what place values on prayers:

(i) Prayers are known to be answered when there is divine intervention as citizens have experienced miracles taking in Nigeria.

(ii) Prayers are perceived to have been answered when the people are given directions on how to solve some problems like the cases of COVID-19 and Ebola crisis. During Ebola crisis, a Nigerian physician called Ameyo Adadevoh with other Doctors stopped the virus from spreading in Nigeria. She detained a Liberian called Patrick Sawyer who was probably sent to spread the virus for whatever reason, going by the way he was eager to leave the hospital. Adadevoh died on 19

Dr. Ameyo Adadevoh

August 2014 of the disease which she stopped from spreading.

(iii) Prayers are also believed to be answered when people get ideas on how to increase the wealth of the nation, make life comfortable for the people or capture the undesirable elements that use diabolical means to terrorize members of the society or community.

(iv) Prayers are also valuable because it can positively shape the National Psyche through consciousness that if they are to get God involved in anything, they have to live and behave right. This is observed when some Christians and Muslims are in their fasting and praying periods. Most of them always behave right at these periods.

Help Us To Build A Nation: Because of the belief in God and that he created all things, the people know that he can build the nation and make it beautiful and habitable where just as the next line indicates, no one is oppressed. If the belief that God is to build the nation exists in the people, it is also assumed that God is to inspire them to move the nation forward. This line of nation building is so crucial that it also reflects in the second stanza of the old anthem as in the line: "To build a nation where peace". This prayer: "Help us to build a nation" is crucial for the following reasons, going by the analogy of the two anthems:

(I) God creates individuals for different purposes. His commitments to mankind makes him to provide all they need such as rain, air, sun and other things which they need before stay alive and fulfil their purposes.

(ii) Just as God is committed to the people by ensuring that they enjoy life to its fullness, everybody is expected to be committed to him by taking good care of his creations, including human beings. Leaders must be committed to the followers by putting their interests into considerations while parents must put the interest of their children and their future ahead of

The Oppressors And The Oppressed

theirs. Failure to do this will amount to misplacement of commitments, which can violate the law of orderliness of God, bringing about confusions; chaos and conflicts.

(iii) Individuals are also made to be committed to one another by being one another's keepers. All Nigerian children must be seen as the future of the nation. Thus they can be blessings or curses to the nation, depending on how they are raised. There were many occasions in Nigeria when parents failed in their responsibilities to their children who later grow into armed-robbers, kidnappers and other criminals that terrorize the nation. If all Nigerian adults do not see all Nigerian children as part of their future, they will teach or allow them to learn wrong things, making them to grow into nuisances that will terrorize the nation years later. Youths who do not fit into the National Value System are the ones involved in terrorism, cultism and hooliganism. They organize or join vice rings or group of criminals that pose threats to the peace of the nation in order to be relevant. This often results into their untimely deaths as it is observed nowadays.

Where No Man Is Oppressed: This line also reflectes in the old national anthem in the first stanza that reads: "One nation bound in freedom." The two indicate that if one is not free, he or she is oppressed.

The Oppressed Child Who Is Supposed To Be In School, Building His Future

Every oppressed person is a slave and the oppressor is the taskmaster. The oppression of any citizen in the society is the oppression of the nation. This line is to ensure that no one is oppressed and no oppressor is allowed. These are the consequences of any nation that is oppressed either by the leaders or by another country, going by historical facts:

Oppressive Government's Power In Action

(I) The citizens of any oppressed

nation is bound to revolt one day. The Apartheid System Of Government in South Africa between 1948 and 1991, which was a racial segregation under the rulership of white minority brought about oppression of the blacks. The result of that was constant violence and mass murder of blacks that are ready to die for their freedom.

Child Oppressor Who Is Trained To Waste Human Lives

(ii) Any oppressed nation would take steps towards regression instead of progression. Oppression of the people destroys their abilities to move the nation forward either economically, socially or politically.

(iii) Crimes and vices are always on the increase in any nation that is oppressed. This is due to the fact that the value systems, including family; moral and traditional values would have been eroded. For this reason, while raising youths that would be used to oppressed the people in future, Vladimir Lenin, the Russian dictator said, "the best revolutionists are youth devoid of morals."

Before considering what can result into the oppression of the nation, it is instructive to note that most people do not seem to care how a leader assume authority or leadership position as long as he or she meets up to their expectations. Thus what can result into oppressions of the people are as follows:

(I) Unpatriotic attitudes or crimes of leaders like political, religious; traditional and community leaders, especially the ones that failed to put the interests of the people ahead of his or hers. For instance a former Governor who was defiant of financial crime agency that accused him of embezzling of eighty-four billions naira which he could have used to build the future of the citizens in the State.

(ii) Ignorance of either the leaders or the followers or of both of them. A lot of people assume leadership positions without the slightest idea of how to lead. Apart from that, they lack information about the needs of the people they are leading. Thus they do not know how to meet these needs.

(iii) Selfishness or self interest which can be defined as lack of considerations for others motivates most people to contest for leadership positions. From observations, leaders who lack considerations for others always oppress the followers in order to get what they want.

(iv) Arrogance often times makes it hard for many people in authority to learn, especially from those who are more experienced than them. Arrogant leaders often do not care who is oppressed under their leadership. Arrogant people always feel that when they assume authority, they are above others. If anyone tries to challenge their authorities in any way, they tend to oppress the person with their powers.

The antidotes to oppressions of citizens by their leaders, especially political leaders are as follows:

(I) Although intelligence is not enough to make good leadership but it is one of the greatest hallmarks that characterizes good leaders. Plato rightly observed that one of the penalties for you (intelligent people) not getting involved in politics (leadership positions) is to be governed by your (their) Inferior. Thus if intelligent people do not bid or contest for leadership positions, fools (intellectually inferior people) will find their ways there either for financial incentives or the prestige that goes along with them. If fools are in positions of power as Nigeria had experienced it over the years, every sector within the nation or organization or institution takes a nose dive into various levels of catastrophes, including political and economic disasters. The reason is that intelligent crooks in the society will find it easy to use the fool in power to their advantages. In other words, the fool in power is an ideal tool in the hands of crooks to oppress the people.

(ii) Another thing that can be attributed to good leadership is good and positive attitudes of the leaders which can always be assessed through their reputations. A lot of Nigerians who are known as criminals often times assumed the positions of authorities. Many people erroneously believe that politics is a dirty game. Politics actually becomes dirty only if dirty people are allowed to make it dirty. It is through political activities that people elect their political leaders. If leaders are dirty, the society would be dirty. The question is: if everywhere is dirty, who would be clean? In fact, no matter how clean a person may try to be, he would be made dirty if he goes into politics that had been made dirty by dirty people. Take for instance a State that owns the workers for well over a year simply because the Governor was dirty enough to embezzle the State fund. What should be expected in a State like that is for the filth to spread to every section in the State, starting from the Civil Service. This is what often leads to briberies, corruptions and other things that will work against the progress of the State. No matter how clean a person maybe, if he is confronted with a situation like this; he would be forced to bend or compromise his principles. Now people may wonder if it is possible to have a clean leader. It is possible if Uruguay can have a president like Jose Mujica since 2010. He was considered the poorest but the best President in the world. What earned his position? He donates 90% of his salary to charity. When he felt sick, he waited in line in the public hospital before he could see the doctor. This man is actually teaching the world what clean politics and services to the nation are all about.

Uruguay President Jose Mujica Waited To See The Doctor In A Public Hospital When He Was Sick - A Good Example Of Good Leadership

(iii) Humility is not only part of good and positive attitude of a leader

Hardworking Nigerians Whose Patriotic Spirits Are Dampened By Some Unpatriotic Leaders

but also an outstanding virtue that characterizes good leadership in all walks of life; including politics, business, community, family and religion. This virtue makes a leader teachable, attentive and sympathetic to the plights of others. Many leaders seem to possess this virtue while vying for leadership positions but soon after they are elected, they become arrogant.

With People And Without Plenty Food, Citizens Will Seem Like Refugees In Their own Country.

(iv) Firm leadership is also required to serve as antidote to oppression of the people. Being humble does not mean the leader should not take his stand when he or she has to. As it is in the nature of man to seek to control many things; including what he lacks the ability to control, many people always attempt to control the leaders. Also most people in powers all over the world do not want to release powers to others even after another person had been elected or selected to lead. Leaders must strictly follow the law and order like the constitution that guides the society or the regulation that regulate the organization. Political leaders in powers are expected to exercise their constitutional authority to lead the nation even in the face of fierce oppositions without fear and without abusing their powers. A weak administration in any given country is vulnerable to corruption and compromise on principles of law, thereby exposing the citizens to oppression.

(v) The leaders must be disciplined because it takes disciplined leaders to discipline others. Without discipline in the society, lawlessness would be on the increase. Without force of the law, vices and crimes would be on the increase. Discipline increases productivity of labour and effectiveness of knowledge acquisition of students in schools.

(vi) Kindness and tolerance of the leadership and the citizens. It must be embedded in everybody of the need to make sacrifices for the good of the society and for others. Thus the people do not need to place price tag on everything they do for the good of others, especially those who cannot afford to pay for the services. Most Nigerians, as it is observed, are not ready to do anything good for free. They always find it hard to work without incentives. In fact, a lot of citizens, including most leaders benefit from the bad systems such as unstable economy and dirty politics that urgently needs to be restored into good condition as indicated in the story about Generational Ship. With this attitude, it becomes very hard if not impossible to do things that would be beneficial to others or the nation without the beneficiaries having to pay for them.

And So With People And Plenty: Again, you will note the similarity between this line of the new and the second stanza of the old anthems, which is "To Build A Nation Where Peace And Justice Shall Reign." This implies that the two anthems recognize the fact that "Where No Man Is Oppressed" as in new or when "One Nation Is Bound In Freedom" as in old anthem, there would be enough to feed the present and the future citizens of Nigeria. Where people are "oppressed" or not "bound in freedom", however, there would be no peace in the society and there would be lack, according to the new anthem and "peace and justice" cannot reign, according to the old anthem. In other words, the followings are the results of peace in the society:

(i) There would be enough workforce of people who are not and whose future are not threatened by oppression of either the Government or other things.

(ii) People whose environment is characterized with peace are often contended people, especially when they consider the price of conflicts and wars. More

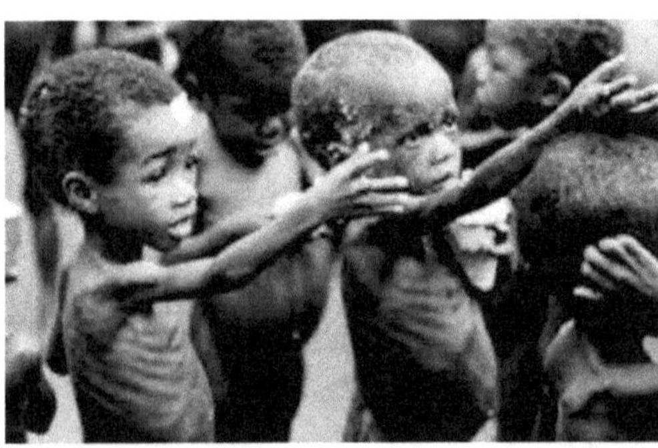

These Children Are Probably Born Under Oppressive Government In The Nation That Is Characterized With Hunger And Sufferings. Their Parents Are Probably Those Who Did Nothing About The Future Of The Children Before They Were Born

often than not, people go into war when their lives, peace or freedom are under attack or serious threats.

(iii) The peace in the nation can bring about stability in the political, economic and social infrastructures and machineries. Citizens tend to feel so insecure when their peace are under threats. Insecurities make them to behave in some irrational ways, including taking laws into their hands. When they go that far, civil unrest or civil other wars is in the making. People only know when wars begin, they do not know when it will end and no one knows what it will cost the nation in terms of lives and properties. For this reasons, John F Kennedy said that mankind must put an end to war before war put an end to mankind. Similarly, any nation which does not prevent civil war by informing the citizens that it is in their interest to preserve Law and Order will lose what it cannot afford to lose, including lives which will take a long time to recover. A very good example is the inability of Nigeria to recover from its loses during civil war that broke out in 1967.

Nigeria May Be Blessed: This line of the new national anthem recognizes the fact that the country can only be truly blessed if everybody identifies his or her roles and plays it accordingly. The followings are the expected roles to be played by all Nigerians before they can be truly blessed by God of all creations whom they believe, going by the two national anthems:

(1) The cause of the nation must be appreciated and respected through deeds and what is taught everywhere in Nigeria, including schools.

(2) All Nigerian citizens must see all the land as their native land without giving any room for ethnic strife, which can result into division. Division is the mother of conflicts, which can blow into full scale civil war. A Nigerian from the North can claim to be from or can be born in the South and vice versa.

(3) No matter their differences either in languages or tribes, citizens must see themselves as brothers and sisters. If they see themselves as the same family, they will feel the need to keep and protect one another against enemies from within or outside Nigeria since a country that is divided against itself cannot stand.

(4) Nigerians must be ready and proud to serve Nigeria which is their sovereign motherland.

(5) With the flag which symbolizes peace and abundance, all Nigerians must always stand together for truth and justice and be ready to embed the same in the minds of their children instead of considering one another as enemies. By considering themselves as enemies or their differences, they work against their own interests, the future and the unity of the nation.

(6) Nigerians must be ready to sacrifice anything for the peace of their country and then expect honour through the act of sacrifice.

(7) Nigerians must be ready to hand over good legacy to their children, who in turn must be ready to hand over the same good legacy like a banner without stain to their own children when they become adults

(8) With the help of God, Nigerians must be ready to build the nation through their contributions into the economy, politics, welfare, education and other things that will make life meaningful to others.

(9) No Nigerian must feel superior or inferior to others because these two complexities can make one the oppressor and the other the oppressed. Any slightest trace of oppression can serve as bacteria that threaten the entire National Value System.

(10) Finally, all Nigerians must strive to be at peace with one another, including citizens who act as enemies.

The above is the analysis of the new national anthem and its comparison with the old anthem.

Let us now study the old national anthem in relation to the National Value System as it is expected to shape the psyches of those who were born between 1978 and 2024 when it was what changed.

THE OLD NATIONAL ANTHEM

The old national anthem of Nigeria was adopted in 1978. Unlike the reinstated anthem which is now the new one, the lyrics of the old one was not composed by one person. Wordings of the old national anthem were combinations of words and phrases taken from five of the best entries in a nation contest. The lyrics were composed into a music by the Nigerian Police Band under the directorship of Benedict E.

Odiase while the lyrics are extracted from the entries of John A. Ilechukwu, Eme Etim Akpan, B. A Ogunnaike, Sota Omoigui and P.O Aderibigbe.

The analysis of the old national anthem is one of the proofs that there are fine poets in Nigeria. It is also a good contribution to the Nigerian Value System, going by the analysis.

The old national anthem goes thus:

Arise, o compatriots,
Nigerian's call obey
To serve our fatherland
With love and strength and faith
The labour of our heroes' past
Shall never be in vain
To serve with heart and might
One nation bound in freedom,
Peace and unity

Oh God of creation,
Direct our noble cause
Guide our leaders right
Help our youths the truth to know
In love and honesty to grow
And living just and true
Great lofty heights attain
To build the nation where peace
And justice shall reign

THE ANALYSIS OF THE OLD NATIONAL ANTHEM:

Arise, O Compatriots: The first line begins with someone who seems to call the attentions of the citizens (compatriots) to the tasks ahead of them. Citizens whose attentions are called this way probably need to be informed of the things which may be of national interests either because they are unconscious of them or oblivious of the implications of neglecting them. By asking all citizens to "arise", the line tries to wake Nigerians up or make them meet up to their responsibilities as citizens.

Nigeria's Call Obey: This line reveals the identity of the person that calls as the nation of Nigeria. In essence, the nation assumes the position of authority. With this authority, everybody is expected to obey the call without hesitation like in the army, especially when it is for important or urgent purposes or both. This call, in whichever way it comes, must be obeyed. This call applies to all citizens, not only the Nigerian soldiers. Sometimes it comes through the children who count on adults to protect them from danger. If the person does not obey the call, it can amount into a crime. Thus, both Criminal and Civil laws indicate that an omission or commission can constitute an offence or a crime. For instance, a man who sees a child taking poison which the man knows can kill him would be held responsible for whatever happens to the child if he does not stop him from taking it. Nigeria's call to be obeyed are in the following ways:

1. All Nigerians are mandated to carry out their civic duties and responsibilities such as reporting any criminal activity around them to the police or doing all they can to help those who are in danger.
2. All Nigerians are mandated to abide by the law, including State and Federal laws. They are also mandated to abide by the rules and order within their communities or organizations where they work or institutions or schools where they are students or in other places that are legally constituted. Violation of any State or Federal laws often constitutes a crime which the State Prosecutor can prosecute.
3. All Nigerians are also mandated not to give room for offence against each other such as breach of contract and others that are actionable under either Contract, Marriage and or other civil laws.

To Serve Our Fatherland: Although this line seems to be woven with the next line of the anthem but the services to the fatherland called Nigeria has more than what it seems. Thus the services to Nigeria include though not limited to the followings:

(1) Complete obedience to the law of fatherland, including Constitutional, Criminal and other laws.

(2) Serving the nation through one way or the other as may be demanded by the law such as the National Youth Service Corps who sometimes are called to assist in the electoral process of electing leaders.

(3) Serving the nation through community development or by educating other citizens of things of national interests. Since no Government in the world can meet all the needs of its people, citizens are needed to contribute in cash or kind into the society for the good of others. This can be regarded as civil or corporate social responsibilities and moral obligations.

With Love And Strength And Faith: Just as in the pledge to Nigeria which is meant to characterize Nigerians to be faithful; loyal and honest people, this line of the national anthem aims at making citizens to be loving, full of strength and faith. The followings depict the attributes that are intended by this line:

(i) Love: This is the greatest of all characteristics in a person. Love is usually a two-way street that exists between two or more people. Love is what brings two persons together and raise a family. Love is what keep the family members together. It is the same love that keeps families together as a community. Love keeps the communities that constitute a state or nation together as one. This love of the fatherland must not be compromised if the country is to survive as a nation. A nation that is devoid of love cannot stand because it would be characterized with hatred and malice which give births to struggles and battles. It is love of the fatherland that made so many soldiers to die during the civil war that broke out in 1967. Love is not just in what people say but also in what they do and what they are ready to sacrifice.

(ii) Strength: It is love of something or someone that gives people the strength to get that thing that is loved or to make sacrifices for the loved ones. If fallen heroes did not love their fatherland to the point of death, where would they get the strength to fight for the unity of Nigeria? Strength which the anthem is trying to depict is in the following terms: (a) Serving the nation with passion and determination (b) serving the nation sacrificially with whatever is available and (C) serving the nation without expecting anything in return but with the hope that others would benefit from the sacrifice. Nigeria is still united today because some people paid the sacrifices to keep it united.

(iii) Faith: This line would be explained in the pledge to Nigeria but it is worthy to note that many people become criminals today, not because they want to constitute problems to the nation. They become criminals because they lost their faith either in the leaders or their parents or the nation as a whole. What all Nigerians must understand is the rationale behind what Edmund Burke said, which is: the only thing necessary for the triumph of evils is for good people to do nothing. In other words, if good people do not love their country to the extent of sacrificing all they can so as to secure the future, the evil that men do will not only live after their deaths but can also destroy every good thing others have achieved, thereby creating a society of evil citizens.

The Labour Of Our Heroes' Past: This line reminds Nigerians of those who have sacrificed so much, including their lives so that the citizens will enjoy the peace in the country. Any nation that had been through civil war will understand what it costs to fight battles. Thus there is need to study the history of Nigeria so as to appreciate the sacrifices of the past heroes. They will also understand the mistakes of past leaders and be well informed about their country. "The labour of our heroes' past" can be depicted in terms of the heroes' tussle over the wealth of the nation, the struggle to keep it save, the battle to make citizens be at peace with one another and to keep the unity of Nigeria.

Shall Never Be In Vain: This line is aimed at reminding Nigerians that the tussles, the struggles and the battles of the past heroes must not be allowed to be in vain. All these heroes in the past are either dead or too old or invalid to do anything again. In other words, they have given all they could and these sacrifices must not be in vain.

To Serve With Heart And Might: This line challenges all Nigerians to serve their nation with hearts and might since this is what the past heroes did, going by the history of the civil war. Unless Nigerians love their fatherland; which gives them strength and faith in Nigeria, they may not be able to serve with their hearts and might. Serving with heart is synonymous with passion to serve while might is using available material resources, talents; physical and mental abilities of the citizens. Any Nigerian who uses his or her position or the available resources to serve his or her interest is not serving the nation. Anyone who uses his or her resources, including talents or position to incite or mislead the people either through entertainments or education or other methods, thereby encouraging crimes or social vices breaks the law. He maybe found guilty as the offenders.

One Nation Bound In Freedom: This line makes it clear that if every Nigerian selflessly serves the nation with heart and might, the society will be free. A nation that is bound in freedom will have its citizens free from the followings:

(i) Freedom from dictatorship type of Government or Colonial masters.

(ii) Freedom from conflicts of interests, especially the one that can result into tussles of powers or struggles for freedom or battles like civil wars.

(iii) Freedom from social vices and crimes which often pose threats to lives and properties, creating security challenges.

Peace And Unity: Although this aspect had been explained in the new anthem but it is instructive to note that the peace and unity of any nation has their price tags, going by historical backgrounds of many nations, including Nigeria. Without making the necessary sacrifices, peace and unity is nearly impossible. The reason is that there are many things that can threaten the peace and unity of a nation. The commonest of those things are as follow:

(i) By nature, man often seeks power to control. Everybody wants to be in charge of everything, especially what concerns him or her. Both parents want to control each other and their children. Their children also want to control their parents and teachers. Government wants to control citizens while citizens want to control the Government. So most people seek the power to control, including going diabolical. The laws, therefore, are enacted to regulate the conduct of everybody, including the leaders.

(ii) When most leaders get to the positions of authority either through force or electoral or other means, they often times disregard what the law says.

(iii) Another threat is sometimes caused by ignorance or negligence or arrogance of some leaders who are unfit to navigate the collective efforts of the citizens to the "noble cause". When the citizens, especially the radicals among them see this weakness of the leaders, they begin to incite the people against the Government, mostly with the objective of getting the power to control. This often leads to rebellion that threatens the peace and unity of the nation.

(iv) Another threats to peace and unity of the nation are vices and crimes. All nations in the world are vulnerable to vices and crimes. The reasons includes the fact that while some people use societal vices and crimes to enrich themselves or gain power, others are simply sadistic enough to get involved in terrorism, ritualism or hooliganism. For the sake of peace and unity, the laws are enacted to regulate conduct of citizens and sanction anyone who breaks any of them.

Oh God Of Creation: Just like the new national anthem, this line of the second stanza indicates that Nigeria as a nation officially recognizes the belief in God and acknowledges him as the creator of all creations. This aspect of belief in God also reflects in the pledge to Nigeria, which would be explained later.

Direct Our Noble Cause: With the belief in God, this line encourages Nigerians to always ask God for direction in their collective efforts towards the noble cause which includes, but not limited to the followings:

1. The quest to bake the national cake for the good of old, young and future generation with everyone getting his or her fair share as it is explained in the introduction of the book.
2. To help in the healing process of the fatherland which is infected with deadly bacteria which can be considered as vices and crimes in the society. These bacteria are deadly enough to either knock down the whole system in the country or destroy it completely.
3. To pursue peace and unity of the nation as indicated in the pledge to Nigeria. This encourages citizens to be their brothers' keepers, or to seek for leadership positions with the aim to serve the people and not to be served.
4. To fulfill the promises which all citizens have made to the nation through the pledge to Nigeria at any point of their lives.

Guide Our Leaders Right: This line recognizes the need to pray for leaders because, more often than not, they are the authors of tales of woes of every nation. When the head is good, other parts of the body will perform well. If it is bad, every part would malfunction. The reasons leaders need to be by guided by God, going by historical facts are as follow:

1. Leaders are human being just like the citizens. Thus they are prone of human errors. Human error sometimes affect the generations yet unborn as it is experienced in Nigeria where the wealth of the nation was mismanaged and made indebted to other nations through loans, which extend from one generation to another. Thomas Jefferson said, "loading up the nation with debts and leaving it for the following generations to pay is morally irresponsible. Excessive debt is a means by which governments oppress the people and waste their substance. No nation has a right to contract debt for periods longer than the majority contracting it can expect to live."
2. Leaders need guidance of God in decision making, especially the one that involves going into war with another country. Making wrong decisions have cost the wealth of some countries and millions of lives of citizens of many nations as in the case of second world war.
3. Other reasons the nation needs God's guidance also include safeguarding the lives of the leaders. As it is observed in Nigeria, some good Governments are not always given chance to build the nation as they desired before ambitious and selfish people overthrow them. Bad government, however, often seems to know how to remain in power for a very long time. The more bad government remains in power, the more good things are destroyed and replaced with bad things.

Help Our Youth The Truth To Know: This line is a prayer to God and also a recognition of the fact that without truth, youth may see good things as bad, bad things as good. Without truth, those who are supposed to be looked up behind bars would be celebrated and sometimes given chieftaincy and religious titles. Without truth, youths may sacrifice their future for the present gains. Truths which youths need to know about their countries, include but not limited to the followings:

(i) Most people, including their leaders all over the world often live by lies; deceptions and manipulations. Although it must be admitted that there are things that need to be kept secret but most of the things that are concealed in secrecy are supposed to be revealed to the public. It is truth that reveals the true identities of those who are to be chosen to lead in any area of life, including business, politics and religion.

(ii) It is truth that empowers everybody, especially the youths who can easily be deceived and used by other people to achieve their illicit or evil desires. Many youths are made to be involved in things that can destroy them, going by results of various research works. Most inmates in Nigerian prisons are youths or middle aged people who have wasted their youthful periods and available resources instead of them to contribute them into the "noble cause" of the nation. If they had known the truth about their conduct, according to those who were interviewed, they would not get involved in what would land them in prisons.

(iii) Youths also need to know the truth so that their lives and that of their children in future can be protected. Obviously, if youths are ignorance of the truth about basic things about life, they will constitute nuisance instead of being relevant in the society. A lot of Nigerian youths in modern days had been lured by those they befriend to places they were used as ritual sacrifices. These who do not know the implication of such crimes often grow into terrorists as it is common in the society.

<u>In Love And Honesty To Grow</u>: This line is teaching every citizen, especially youths to grow in love because only through this way they can tolerate one another. They are also taught to grow into honest citizens because without honesty, corruption which sometimes begins with students cheating during examination will set in.

<u>And Living Just And True</u>: This line of the anthem is also a request to God to make Nigerian youths to live just and true life. It also recognizes the fact that the knowledge of the truth in the preceding line (Help Our Youth The Truth To Know) helps to live just and true life. The word "just" can be explained as being moral, responsible and reasonable. While the word "true" in this context means real. Thus this line can be explained in line with the previous lines, saying that God should help Nigerian youths to understand that the real life of a Nigerian must be lived in moral, reasonable and responsible ways. Apart from knowing the truth, other things that can help youth to live just and true life include the followings:

(i) <u>The fear of God</u>. This makes a person God-fearing. Going by histories of various countries that had been studied, nations which do not officially recognize the belief in God is vulnerable to vices and crimes as earlier indicated in the new anthem.

(ii) The love for humanity: This is also important in making the people to live just and true life. As Karl Marx once observed when he said "religion is the opium of the people", the belief in the gods that demand for blood of fellow human beings can be used to cause catastrophe in the society. The love for humanity, however, can counter such belief and possibly make them understand that "God Of Creation" will never instruct anyone to destroy his work, let alone to kill fellow human beings for whatever reasons. In other words, the love for humanity will hold the notion that "you do to others what you would have them to do to you."

(iii) The Belief In The Value System: This system which is embedded in the new and old national anthem and the pledge to Nigeria is enforced by the laws, making citizens live just and true. If youths are conscious of the fact that all their actions either good or bad have consequences, they will live right. From the interviews which the author of this book have conducted with some inmates in different prisons in Nigeria, most of them either do not know nor believe that their conduct will land them in jail. While vast majority of children and youths are not educated or informed about Nigerian value system by their teachers, some do not even know anything about the value system. Others who know about it deliberately violate it because of the incentives they find in vices and crimes. When they are faced with the consequences of their actions, they begin to look for people like their parents and government to blame.

Great Lofty Heights Attain: This line is also a request to God Of Creation, praying that through the youths, Nigeria will attain great and lofty heights, which connotes great achievements in various walks of life such as Medicine; Engineering, Law, Politics, Education,

Moving Up On The Ladder Of Life May Not Be An Easy Task But The Youth Who Patiently Takes One Step After The Other Will Easily Move Up

Humanity, Character Building professions and other areas. However, there is no way anyone can attain any of these heights without following these basic principles, which can be studied in one of the author's books titled "Building Your Future And The Nation Now". They are as follow:

1. Youths must appreciate the value of time. In other words, they need to understand that they must spend time to enhance their value in life by getting educated or starting to acquire experiences in their chosen careers instead of wasting it on pleasures. Any of their hours that is wasted is a part of their lives that is wasted, which may not be recovered.
2. They must not give up in their efforts to achieve great things in life, knowing fully well that there are many others, including their families that would benefit from their efforts.
3. They must never be lazy. Any lazy person cannot go beyond the ground level of the "Great Lofty Heights".
4. They must live a simple life instead of complicated or double life.
5. They must be honest in their dealings, according to the pledge they make to Nigeria. A dishonest person is either a nuisance in the society or a rogue that stains the names of his or her family, community and the nation.
6. They must be kind to fellow citizens so that they may also receive the same treatment. Human beings are usually the reflections of whom we are in the inside. As a kind person often seems to be surrounded by kind persons, wicked people often seem surrounded by wicked people. That is the reason the adage says a murderer would not give room for anyone to play with sword around him. The reason, of course, is that he is always suspicious that someone maybe planning to kill him just as has killed others.
7. Youths must never shun their responsibilities and duties to the nation, their families and fellow citizens.
8. They must be judicious in their spending. Since they are still depending on other people, every amount of money they get must be invested in themselves or their future such as building their careers or getting trained in their chosen professions.
9. To attain a great and lofty heights in life, it takes time and lots of efforts. So youths who want to reach the peak of their

careers in life must be very patient. Those who tries to take short cuts always shortens their successes and most times their lives. This accounts for the rate at which youths of nowadays are losing their lives. The outcome of research works indicates that impatience often makes youths to cut corners, making them to either end up in prisons or lose their lives.

10. Finally, youths must always acquire and improve on their skills. Through that, they enhance their value.

To Build A Nation: When youths of any society makes efforts to enhance their value in life by following the above principles, the nation will be well built on a solid foundation. If the youths do not build themselves, they will destroy the existing infrastructures to build the economy, political and other systems in the society. According to the book: "Building Your future And The Nation Now," the wealth of a nation is not in its financial, natural or other resources but rather in the attitudes of the citizens of the country. In other words, attitudes of the citizens are either the assets that bring blessings or burdens that brings pains and sorrow to the nation. For this reason, one of the American greatest Presidents, John Kennedy told American citizens when their country was faced with challenges, "think of what you can do for your country, not what the country will do for you." Citizens do not build a nation by placing demand on the nation. Thus youths need to think of how to build the nation by making efforts to build themselves into patriotic, responsible, reasonable and successful members who allows other citizens to benefit from their

One Of The Best Ways To Build A Nation Is To Build The Children. Children That Are Not Built Will Either Become Destitute Or Threats To Lives And Properties

Kidnappers That Hold Expatriates To A Ransom - Part Of The Proofs Of The Near Extinction Of The Nigerian Value System

efforts. When they do this, they will earn the respects of members of the society who can elect them as their leaders.

Where Peace And Justice Shall Reign: This line emphasizes the fact that peace and justice can only reign when the above steps are taken and the pledges that are made to Nigeria are fulfilled. The point in this line is explained in the new anthem under the headings of: "That Truth And Justice Reign" and "In Peace Or Battle honoured"

Having explained the new national anthem, it is also vital to explain the pledge to Nigeria so that every Nigerian may understand the implications of breaking it

THE PLEDGE TO NIGERIA

I Pledge To Nigeria, My Country: This pledge or promise is very crucial for all Nigerians to make to the nation because it makes them very conscious of what the law says as it reflects in the new and old national anthems, making them obedient and committed to the society at the early stages of their lives.

To Be Faithful, Loyal And Honest: These three great virtues need to characterize every Nigerian who at least passes through Primary School because most, if not all of them would one day become either Parents or Family Heads or Community or Political or other Leaders in future:

(I) Faithfulness: This is meant to characterize Nigerians as faithful people who believe in the cause and purpose of the nation, making them reasonable, responsible and law-abiding citizens. It is also important for all Nigerians to be faithful, especially in the things that are of national interest because unfaithfulness gives room for malpractice that ranges from cheating during examination to electoral fraud. Any act of unfaithfulness is a violation of this pledge, which can amount to a crime.

(II) Loyalty: This attribute needs to be embedded in all Nigerians because history indicates that the levels of loyalties of the citizens of every society are often tested in the time of crisis, where sometimes people are tempted to allow personal interests to take precedence over national interest. By and large, the pledge makes disloyalty to the nation an outright betrayal which can amount to Felony or Treason like cases of coup d'etat which set Nigeria backward.

(III) Honesty: This aspect of The Pledge To Nigeria is meant to teach all Nigerians to be honest in all their dealings either in politics or business or other things. Any act of dishonesty in a society or organization or institution can cause a stain in the reputation of the people within. There was a time when Nigerians who were applying for visas to other countries would have to prove that they not fraudulent because they are not trusted. The Police, Civil Servants and other people were assumed to be dishonest by other countries because of fraudulent practice that was common till now. The author of this book had the experience of how a stain in the reputation of the nation could feel like when his book was about to be published in USA. The publishers wanted him to prove it to them that he is the owner of the intellectual property that was submitted to them for publication. The reason, according to them, was that the US Government back then have warned them to be very careful in the way they dealt with Nigerians. This so provoked the author that he told them that he would rather prove it to them that there were more criminals in US than in Nigeria than to prove that he is the author. He cancelled the deal with the publishers.

To Serve Nigeria With All My Strength: This line implies the total commitments of all Nigerians to the good of the nation by carrying out their duties and responsibilities in this order of priority:

(a) To The Nation

(b) To Their Families and

(c)To Fellow Nigerians.

If this order is misplaced, there would be conflicts of interests, which can result into chain of reactions, including divisions. Divisions can cause conflicts, which can result into breaking the law.

To Defend Her Unity: This line Is a cord that holds all Nigerians together despite their differences in languages, customs, religions and lifestyles.

Without the mind to defend the unity of Nigeria, there would be conflicts and divisions like the one that almost caused the nation to break into different countries during the civil war. To defend the unity of Nigeria, the people must never dwell on the differences in their interests, religions, cultures, lifestyles and other things. They should dwell on common grounds like the constitution that guarantees every Nigerian's fundamental human rights.

Uphold Her Honour And Glory: It is honourable attitude that brings glory to a nation. Dishonourable attitudes of Nigerians, especially political, religious and other leaders bring shame and dishonour to the country. Upholding the honour and glory of any country lies in the patriotic attitudes of both leaders and the citizens of Nigeria.

So Help Me God: This line just as it is indicated and explained in both new and old national anthems, recognizes the fact that there are forms of beliefs in God in virtually all norms and cultures that constitute the Nigerian Value System. Invariably, this line of The Pledge makes most Nigerians believe there is God and this may characterize them as religious people. Although Karl Marx may seem to be right when he said, "religion is the opium of the people," especially if we consider how it had been used to cause crises in Nigeria, but if we study the horrifying effects of a nation that never officially believe in God as influenced by people like Karl Marx and Lenin, we would conclude that a Godless nation is vulnerable to all sorts of crimes and evils, including terrorism. Atheistic theories of such people have created more catastrophes in the history of man than anything good as it is observed in some countries like Russia. While building on Karl Marx theories, Lenin said that the best revolutionists are youths devoid of morals. Going by the study of his activities and that of his successor, Joseph Stalin, revolutionists were people whose ideas agreed with theirs though they may be murderous while their enemies were those who disagreed with them in any way. This is what accounted for the mass murder of millions of Russians.

Religion, however, can truly become opium of the people to misbehave if it is not made voluntary by reasons of virtues and logics.

Belief in God which needs to be influenced by reasons of

virtues and logics instead of being enforced, plays the following roles in the nation:

I. As earlier indicated, belief in God boosts the moral values of citizens by making them feel that there is God who pays everyone, according to his or her deeds, whether good or bad.

II. Because God is perceived as being capable of bringing judgment upon the people who violate any of his commandments, the belief in God makes them God-fearing. God-fearing people are often law-abiding and responsible citizens.

III. Among other things, belief in God can bring peace, tolerance, joy and harmony within the society.

Any religion which does not play all the above roles must not be encouraged in the society. All religions or groups which pose threats to human lives or properties needs to be wiped out since they contravene the law and order.

Apart from making citizens to understand what Nigeria as a nation stands for and against, giving everybody the true picture of the National Value System, the new and old anthems and the pledge are ways of making every member of the society to master what the law says right from childhood.

CONCLUSION WITH THE STORY OF THE FOUR YOUNG COMPATRIOTS WHO MAKE NIGERIA GREAT

There were four young Compatriots called Promise, Faithful, Loyal and Honest who came from the Eastern, Western, Southern and Northern parts of Nigeria.

When they were in schools, they were made to pledge to serve the nation with all their strengths; to defend her unity; uphold her honour and glory. They knew, however, that they cannot fulfil these pledges without the help of God because of their limitations as youths back then. So they always pray to God of all creations to help them.

They were taught in the school about the National Value System where they realized that failures to keep the pledge they made to Nigeria can result into vices or crimes which can take them to jail or even cause them to lose their lives. They were also made to understand that they were the future of the nation and whatever they did at their young age would determine if they would be useful or useless to their families, communities and the nation at large. If they were disciplined; well-equipped and well-informed for the future, they stand the chances of becoming great leaders in the fields of politics, business, medicine, education and other aspects of life.

With these in mind, they aspired to be the best they could by making best use of the opportunities and resources that were made available to them either by the Government or their families or other people who were willing to support them in their chosen careers.

While they worked hard to fulfil these pledges and enhance their values in life, so many other youths who can be called Indiscipline, Unruly, Heady, Ignorant, Carefree, Selfish, Malicious and Ferocious were busy breaking the pledges they also made to Nigeria. The four young compatriots refused to join the company of these other youths because they know they were on the wrong path. Through the violation of the pledge to the nation, it was apparent to them that the bad gang will soon end up their lives either in prisons or graves.

As part of their services to the nation, the young Compatriots tried to positively influence some bad gang members to be of good behaviour. Some of them changed their ways and joined the good company of Compatriots while the rest form vice rings like secret cults, group of terrorists, fraudsters and other agents of societal problems.

Soon enough, Nigerian motherland which was once peaceful became hostile environment where lives and potentials were either threatened or destroyed. Armed-robberies, sales of parts of human bodies and human trafficking became rampant in the society. The system began to go down with only few trying to bring it back to work. These vices and crimes began to destroy the economic and the political structures, making most people either threatened, sick or tired of living.

The madness in the motherland of Nigerians spread round the nation. This compelled some people to fly out of Nigeria and become third class citizens or illegal immigrants in another country. Many others who cannot leave the country are forced to apply any means to survive, including killing others for money or using their children to steal or flirt around like street dogs.

Still these four Compatriots refused to give up their faith in

God of all creations who gave them strength to sail through the ocean of insanity. Because they love their country, they made lots of sacrifices for her in spite of the fact that they also needed help. They shared their things with other Compatriots who do not have the strength to hang on during this period of crisis. They educated others of the need to be on the side of God.

These Compatriots continued to pray for everybody, including the leaders who seemed confused by what is happening, saying:

"Oh God of all creations
Grant this our one request
Help us to build a nation
Where no man is oppressed,
And so with peace and plenty
Nigeria maybe blessed"

Because of this prayer and because they refused to go crazy like many other people who do crazy things, God begins to prepare them to become reasonable, responsible and patriotic leaders.

Some years later, God used these Compatriots to remove the madness in Nigeria. While some members of the then bad gangs are either dead as a result of their involvements in crimes, some had become beggars who count on others for survivals. Many of them had wasted their productive years in prisons or in doing nothing.

This is the true picture of Nigeria and destinies of young Nigerians. All Nigerians can now decide their future and that of the nation. The decision is not in what they say and think alone but also in what they do.

Young Nigerians have the chance of making their country a better place to stay or leave their destinies in the hands of those who are ready to destroy them.

The final question is: What Is Your Decision? You have to give the final answer. If you have decided to be one of the young Compatriots that would make Nigeria great, you can take another step by reading another of the author's book titled: "Building Your Future And The Nation Now".

For you to also enhance your values in life, you need to study the materials on vices, virtues and values in the seminar and Student Orientation Studies in the next page.

WHAT IS SOCIAL VICES?

For the purpose of this paper, which is designed to enlighten students and not for academic purpose, social vices would be simply described as any act or behaviour that may be considered harmful or deadly to an individual, family, community or the society directly or indirectly. Thus if a person incite or influence another person to harm others or to misbehave, they are both partners in vices or crimes.

WHY VICES ARE HARMFUL OR DEADLY TO THE NATION?

If you think of the number of people or the rate at which the youths, the future of Nigeria are dying as a result of social vices, there may not be need for this question. However for more knowledge, the followings are the most vital reasons:

1. Vices destroy and waste human lives, including participants and youths with bright future and careers. Many promising Nigerians have lost their lives on campus while trying to build their careers as a result of social vices like cultism.
2. Vices can destroy the future; dreams and potentials of individuals, families and the nation. Youths who are enlisted into armed robberies, drug addictions and prostitution sabotage the good things about their lives. A lot of people through vices like sexual promiscuity have been infected and had also infected others with Sexually Transmitted Diseases (STD) while some, through abortions, have lost their lives or abilities to produce children, who are also the future of the nation. Note that some STDs can make a man unable to impregnate a woman. In Africa, if a man's wife is unable to conceive, the woman is often considered barren.
3. Vices destroy good name of families and society at large. The cases of 419 scam have given the nation of Nigeria negative image, making most other countries suspicious of Nigerians. Nigerians are treated like common rogues in some parts of the world.
4. Among other reasons, vices are harmful to the political, economic growths and social life of the people. Such harm includes cyber crimes, armed robberies and assassinations of political figures. Results of research works indicate that vices give birth to all kinds of crimes, including murder and sales of human parts.

REASONS PEOPLE ARE INVOLVED IN SOCIAL VICES

If certain behaviours are considered evil or harmful to the society, why do some people; especially youths get involved? Going by the results of CEMS research works, the followings are most of the reasons:

1. Financial Incentives: Many youths are involved in social vices like prostitution, rituals, blood contract (killing people for money),

armed-robberies and others because of financial gains. When they are caught and made to face the consequences of their misdeeds or crimes, they begin to regret them. The jungle justice which the public inflict on some participants when they were caught and the interviews that were conducted with some inmates prove this as a fact.

2. Peer Group Influence: Many people, especially youths make friends with wrong set of people. Such groups get them involved in social vices. If you do not make friends with right people, wrong people will make you their friends willy-nilly.
3. Quest For Spiritual Powers: Many people often seek for spiritual powers with the belief that it will make them rich or earn them political positions or respects. In the cause of that, they get involved in ritual killings. There is a case study of a young man who went for such powers. He was told to use a charm to hit anyone that was conjured to him in a shrine. When the spirit of the person was conjured, it was his mother. He was afraid to do it but when the witch doctor told him if he did not do it, he would die. He hit the mother, causing her to slump and die while she selling food items in her shop. The young man became rich but later became mad. When he ran mad, he confessed all his deeds.
4. Quest Of Ambitious People For Political Powers: Some people who are ambitious to occupy political positions sometimes use youths to assassinate their rivals. Cases of terrorism are also typical examples of such people who, in order to occupy political posts, make use of youths to terrorize the people in many ways and compel them to clamour for political change.
5. Demand For Attention And Desire For Relevance In The Society: Many youths are involved in social vices because they want to command other people's attentions or respects or to impress their friends or lovers. Some of them who just want to be relevant in their environments go about this by creating fear in the minds of people around them. Series of cases of secret cults on campus and in secondary schools that were studied confirm this fact.
6. Influence Of Media And Entertainment Industries: The influence of all these in addition with technology also forms parts of the reasons youths are involved vices. There some songs and movies that celebrate vices and make crimes look glamourous. Most of the movie themes and music lyrics are designed to brainwash youths and encourage them to get involved in social vices. Symptoms of brainwashed youths can be observed in the way they behave, talk, dress or walk.
7. Adolescent Attitudes And Other Ways Of Proving To Be Matured or Courageous: Most youths, when they get to the age of

adolescence, always want to prove to others that they are grownups. In the cause of doing this, they get involved in social vices. Some go as far as beating up their teachers for trying to discipline them in the schools_as it is observed in some case studies.

CONSEQUENCES OF SOCIAL VICES

Some consequences of vices are treated under why vices are harmful to the nation. Here are few more reasons youths must fight against instead of getting involved in vices or crimes:

(A) Vices and crimes do not contribute into the economy or progress of the nation. Instead they destroy or undermine political and economic growth in the society.

(B) Going by CEMS experiences in prison ministrations, all prisons in Nigeria are getting more and more congested with steady inflow of convicted people, most of whom are youths. This poses challenges of having lots of inmates that depend on Government fund for survival in the prison.

(C) If youths who are supposed to be the future of the nation are kept in prisons, they would not be able to enhance their values in life by going to school or by building their careers. Apart from this, Government would be forced to use the fund that may be used for other things like education to cater for the inmates and also to sustain their healths. Life in prison is in most times a living hell for those who are inside. As an adage says, for every action, there is always reaction one way or the other. If anyone is involved in any vice, he or she may end up in jail when he is to be in school. For this reason CEMS always recommends schools to take their especially unruly students on excursions to prisons.

(D) Another consequences is that people can either become victims or participants in social vices. Life is like a tug of war. If good people do not fight the ills in the society, they will either join bad gang or become their victims. Since none of the options of joining bad gang or becoming its victim is good, people need to begin fighting vices and crimes now.

WAYS TO FIGHT SOCIAL VICES AS NIGERIAN STUDENTS

1. Youths must first understand that their country needs them to fight against vices so as to enjoy peace and harmony in the society now and in future. They must make up their minds never to join bad gangs even if they are not yet fit to fight them. If they join them, they may end up in prison or die young, To better appreciate the reasons they must shun social vices, they need to study the play titled: "Bloodshed In Campus" in page 50. The play is the result of research works on part of the consequences of cultism on campus and in secondary schools. If youths had been influenced to develop unpatriotic attitude, they must change

before it is too late. Positive change in any society is not feasible without the citizens changing their negative attitudes.

2. Youths must also concentrate on enhancing their values in life by focusing on their education and careers. This is very important to them, their families, communities, nation and the entire world. They may be called to lead in any capacities if they live just and true lives as the anthem says. To get knowledge on how to enhance their values, they can study the book titled; "Building Your Future And The Nation Now".
3. Youths must fulfil the pledges they make to the nation because breaking any of them like being unfaithful and disloyal or dishonest to the nation or anyone may result into breaking the law. To understand this further, they need to study the book titled: "The Values of The Two Anthems And The Pledge To Nigeria."
4. Lastly, youths must take their stand or campaign against social vices in every way they can.

Having explained these, there is need for youths and adults to to go through Nigerian Study Orientation Studies.

THE NIGERIAN STUDENT ORIENTATION STUDIES (SOS)

Aims And Objectives Of Students Orientation Studies (SOS)

Value Teachers or School Counsellors are required to organize and coordinate groups of students that may be called by any name for the following purposes:

(1) Gauge the impact of Value Education and Orientation Programmes on students' attitudes in their schools.

(2) Prepare them for future leadership roles and roles of responsible parents.

(3) To engage their minds with extra-curriculum activities that will boost their moral values and virtues, educating them on consequences of their involvements in social vices and crimes.

(4) Disabuse their minds of hate speeches; immoral songs and other things that corrupt the society, guiding them against hostile environment that had been created for them through social media and other means of information and entertainments.

(5) Develop their interests in education and challenge them to become assets to the nation instead of constituting nuisances.

(6) Develop their talents and encourage them to use their gifts for the good of the nation right from tender age.

(7) Inform them of the consequences of failing to fulfil The Pledge To Nigeria and groom them into patriotic, responsible and reasonable parents; citizens and leaders of tomorrow.

STUDENT ORIENTATION STUDY ITEMS

John Kennedy's Quote: *"Think of what you can do for your country, not what the country will do for you."*

Topic: Three Things You Can Do For Nigeria

1. You need to love and serve Nigeria with all your strength by campaigning against vices.
2. You must fulfil the pledge you make to Nigeria.
3. You must have faith in God of creation who would help you and the nation to succeed.

Debate This Issue: Are Nigerians doing all they can to build the nation or not?

Plutarch's Quote: *"The richest soil, uncultivated produces the rankest weeds."*

Topic: Three Things That Can Turn Rich Soil (Natural Resources) Into Rankest Weeds (Vices/Crimes) In Any Nation

1. Greediness and selfishness, which is lack of considerations for others
2. Unpatriotic attitudes like violating the rules and regulations in the society or saying provocative things about the nation.
3. Lack of fear of God of creation.

Debate This Issue: Nigerian good soil is turned into weeds by the leaders or the citizens?

Wole Soyinka's Quote: *"I am convinced that Nigeria would have been more highly developed country without the oil. I wish we'd never smelled the fumes of petroleum."*

Topic: Three Reasons Human Developments Are More Important Than Natural Resources.

1. The skills of the people can turn things like stones into valuable things like the Statue of Liberty in United States.
2. It is lack of brain development that turns valuable things like oil into disasters such as destructions of oil pipelines and other things.
3. It is lack of morals or fear of God of creation that turns people into criminals or terrorists.

Debate This Issue: Is Nigerian Government developing more of natural or more of human resources?

Desmond Tutu's Quote: *"We learn from history (so) that we don't learn from history."*

Topic: Three Things To Learn From History.

1. We learn from the mistakes of those who made history so as not to face the same consequences of the their mistakes.
2. We learn from the good deeds of great people if we also want to be great in life.
3. We learn that if we do the wrong things, we should not expect good results.

Debate This Issue: Do Nigerians learn from mistakes of those who make history or not?

John Lubbock's Quote: *"What we see depends mainly on what we look for."*

Topic: Three Things To Consider Before Looking For Anything In Life

1. If you look for trouble, you will get into trouble.
2. If you see a problem and look for solution, you will get solution that can make you a star.
3. The way you react to problems will tell if you are part of the problem or not.

Debate This Issue: Are Nigerian youths or their parents part of causes of problems in Nigeria?

John Rockefeller's Quote: *"I have made millions but they brought me no peace."*

Topic: Three Things Money Can Cause

1. Money can destroy peace of mind or terminate people's lives if it is not legitimately made.
2. Money can destroy valuable relationships if it is placed ahead of interest of other people.
3. The love of money can cause some people to become wicked enough to terminate lives.

Debate This Issue: What can solve most of the problems in Nigeria between money and positive attitudes?

Zig Ziglar's Quote: *"The poorest of all men is the one without a dream."*

Topic: Three Things That Can Cause Poverty

1. Lack of vision and direction in life.
2. Laziness or lack of interest in working hard.
3. Lack of patience, perseverance and endurance to overcome obstacles.

Debate This Issue: Are Nigerian youths too lazy to work or too impatient to be successful?

John Johnson's Quote: *"Men and women are limited not by the place of their birth, not by colour of their skins but by the size of their hope."*

Topic: Three Enemies Of Success In Life

1. Complete loss of hope in getting success or loss of faith in one's ability to excel.
2. Giving excuses for failures in endeavours.
3. Complaints about available resources or looking up to people for help.

Debate This Issue: Do Nigerians have reasons to be failures or not?

Dipo Toby Alakija's Quote: *"If you really put all you can in building a castle in the air, you will end up building a mansion in a beautiful city."*

Topic: Three Things That Spark Success

1. People that encourage you to be successful in your quests or

careers in life.

2. Your zeal and determination to pursue your success.

3. The relevant information you have about your quests or careers in life.

Debate This Issue: Can youths with visions be frustrated in their efforts to excel or not?

Clarence Munn's Quote: *"The difference between great and good is a little effort."*

Topic: <u>Three Categories Of People</u>

1. The spectators that watch history being made.
2. Famous people that make good history.
3. Notorious people that make bad history.

Debate This Issue: Are Nigerian Governments full of famous or notorious people?

Zig Ziglar's Quote: *"Expect the best. Prepare for the worst. Take what comes."*

Topic: <u>Three Causes Of Failures In Life</u>

1. Fear of what people would say or think if the person fails.
2. Inability to see all failures as experiences to learn or as stepping stones to success in life.
3. Inability to take time to come up with good plans that will work.

Debate This Issue: Are Nigerians suffering because they lack plans or the abilities to implement their plans?

Ralph Waldo Emerson's Quote: *"Believe in yourself, and what others think won't matter."*

Topic: <u>Three Kinds Of Feelings That Affect Life</u>

1. Inferiority complex or feelings of inadequacy.
2. Feelings of rejection by family or friends.
3. Feeling of doubt in one's God-given ability.

Debate This Issue: Which of these feelings can more easily kill youth morales for success between inferiority complex or feelings of rejection by family and friends

Dipo Toby Alakija's Quote In His Book: Bloodshed In Campus: *"If you don't make (good) friends, (bad) friends will make you."*

Topic: <u>Three Things You Have Power To Make</u>

1. You can make good friends who can help you live a just and true life.
2. You can avoid bad friends who are ready to destroy your life.
3. You can make trouble and face the consequences or avoid getting into trouble.

Debate This Issue: Do youths have powers to take their destinies in their own hands or not?

Dipo Toby Alakija's Quote In His Book: Bloodshed In Campus: *"You must understand that if good guys shy away from leadership positions, bad guys will find their way there. The good people would be the ones that would suffer unless they join the bad guys."*

Topic: Three Essential Things In Good Leadership In Nigeria

1. Ability to navigate the collective efforts of the people towards the noble cause of the nation.
2. Faithfulness, loyalty and dedication in serving the people.
3. Transparent honesty of all leaders .

Debate This Issue: Who are responsible for the high level of corruption in Nigeria - Politicians or Civil Servants?

Edmund Burke's Quote: *"The only thing necessary for the triumph of evil is for good men to do nothing. "*

Topic: Three Things To Use Against Vices

1. The collective wills of the people in general.
2. To shun and campaign against any form of vices.
3. To report any form of social vices or crimes to security agencies.

Debate This Issue: Do people need Government every time they want to fight against vices or not?

(Dale Carnegie's Quote: *"Any fool can criticize, condemn, and complain and most fools do. "*

Topic: Three Things To Expect From People With Negative Attitudes.

1. They criticize other people who are trying to archive great things .
2. They condemn others who are celebrated for their achievements out of jealousies.
3. They complain a lot and give excuses or blame others for their failures to archive something.

Debate This Issue: Are people with negative attitudes the causes of failures of others or not?

Gilbert Arland's Quote: *"When an archer misses the mark, he turns and looks for fault within himself. Failure to hit the bull's-eyes is never the fault of the target. To improve on your aim, improve on yourself."*

Topic: Three Things In Archiving Success

1. Self-apprasals and evaluations like areas of strengths, weaknesses and limitations.
2. Improvements of skills and sourcing for opportunities in relation to the main goal.
3. Sourcing and making best use of information.

Debate This Issue: Do attitudes or resources determine the pace of success of people?

John C. Maxwell's Quote: *"A difficult crisis can be readily endured if we retain the conviction that our existence holds a purpose, a cause to pursue, a person to love, a goal to achieve."*

Topic: Three Major Purposes Of Life

1. Life is not meant to be enjoyed at the expense of other people but to be used to please God of creation through services to others.
2. Life is to be shared with family members, loved ones and other people by helping them.
3. Life is not meant to cause trouble but to bring peace to humanity.

Debate This Issue: Can life be more enjoyable with money or with people?

Theodore Epp's Quote: *"Our strength is seen in the things we stand for; our weakness is seen in the things we fall for."*

Topic: Three Common Things In Great People

1. They are so disciplined that they never indulge in pleasure at the expense of their goals.
2. They always endure in the time of crisis till they archive their aims.
3. They are so determined that they hardly see any obstacles on the way to their success.

Debate This Issue: Are great people made or born?

Proverb 24:10: *"If you faint in the day of adversity, your strength is small."*

Topic: Three Common Things In Weak People

1. They are always dependent on others for many things, including their daily needs.
2. If others do not help them for whatever reason, they dislike or complain about them.
3. They fall into temptation to go into social vices or get involved in immoral act like prostitution.

Debate This Issue: Is Government responsible for the great number of weak people in the society or not?

Bulwer Lytton's Quote: *"A good heart is better than all the heads in the world."*

Topic: Three Great Qualities In Good Leadership

1. The attitude of love of the people.
2. Foresight or ability to see ahead of others.
3. Ability to see the plight of the people and handle issues.

Debate This Issue: Where do you have better leadership - State or Federal Government?

Robespierre's Quote: *"No man can climb out beyond the limitations of his own character."*

Topic: Three Things About Character

1. Character proves the strength or weakness of a person.
2. The patriotic or unpatriotic attitudes of citizens determine the wealth of the nation.
3. The attitudes of individuals determine how successful they would be. Many people have destroyed their successes with their attitudes.

Debate This Issue: Can Government determine the successes of individuals or not?

David Brinkleys's Quote: *"A successful man is one who can lay a firm foundation with bricks others have thrown at him."*

Topic: Three Qualities Of People With Potentials For Greatness

1. They never take offence if they are criticized even if they know they are right.

2. They know the difference between constructive and destructive criticisms.
3. They learn from others and allow their works to prove their critics wrong.

Debate This Issue: Is Nigeria full of constructive or destructive critics?

John C. Maxwell's Quote: *"If your vision does not cost you anything, it is daydream."*

Topic: Three Things Your Vision Can Cost You

1. It can cost you all your savings and still require much more before you reach your goal.
2. It can cost you your pride or dignity, especially when you are struggling to carry it out.
3. It can make you to be at loggerheads with your family members and friends when they disagree with you or your vision.

Debate This Issue: Do youths need to fall apart with their parents if they try to kill their visions or not?

Zig Ziglar's Quote: *"Keep trying. It is only from the valley that the mountain seems so high."*

Topic: Three Things That Make Visions Come True

1. The faith in God of creation that He can make it real if the dream is to benefit humanity.
2. Quality time that is spent in planning to implement visions.
3. Hard work and perseverance that will make it hard to give up until the goal is carried out.

Debate This Issue: Is it impatience or lack of faith in God that causes some goals not to be accomplished?

Arthur Friedmen's Quote: *"Men of genius are admired. Men of wealth are envied. Men of power are feared, but only men of character are trusted."*

Topic: Three Things About People Without Character

1. If they are cunning, honest people may not want to be their friends or to deal with them.
2. If they are wealthy, they may be surrounded by crooks who want their wealth by all means.
3. If they are powerful, they may be surrounded by enemies whom they might have hurt or offended with their powers.

Debate This Issue: Is it justified to steal from those who have stolen from the nation or not?

John C Maxwell's Quote: *"Your attitude is either your best friend or your worst enemy, your greatest asset or your greatest liability."*

Topic: Three Things About People With Character

1. They are always trusted with leadership roles if they have other leadership qualities.
2. They always have people trusting them with money or doing business with them.
3. People always take their advice or listen to them when they are

talking about morals.

Debate This Issue: Is good character developed or inherited?

John C Maxwell's Quote: *"Anytime the going seems easier, better check and see if you're not going down the hill."*

Topic: Three Things You Must Note In Progress

1. Moving up in the ladder of success of life is a difficult task.
2. Anyone who attempts to climb the ladder from the top will end up on the ground.
3. Progress in life is determined by experiences and how much you are willing to learn.

Debate This Issue: Does everybody need Government support or not before they can progress in life?

Ralph Waldo Emerson's Quote: *"Our chief want in life is someone to inspire us to be what we really want to be."*

Topic: Three Things To Note About The Person You Want To Pick As Your Role Model.

1. If you pick the wrong person as your role model, you will develop bad attitude or wrong habits such as immoral entertainers who corrupt youths through songs or movies.
2. Your role model can determine what you will become in life - good or bad citizen.
3. Role models can inspire you to be great in life or incite you to take law into your hands through their ways of life.

Debate This Issue: Are Nigerian Youths to be blamed for picking wrong role models or not?

Wills Diamen's Quote: *"Nothing reveals your true nature like a difficulty or a problem."*

Topic: Three Tests Of Strengths Of Character

1. It is during the time of crisis that character strength of individuals can be best tested.
2. The temptation or the situation that compels people to compromise with their stand in any issue is a test of character strength.
3. People who pressurize you to do the wrong instead of right thing is another test.

Debate This Issue: Can people who fail tests of character be blamed for their failures or not?

Ronald M. Evans' Quote: *"To obtain funding, you have to convince people that you're doing something that's important."*

Topic: Three Essential Things To Note Before You Can Get Support For Your Vision Or Idea

1. The vision needs to be beneficial to people if it is implemented.
2. You have no interior or hidden motives behind the idea or vision.
3. You are capable or you have what it takes to implement the vision or the idea.

Debate This Issue: Does Nigerian environment encourages good visions or not?

Dale Carnegie's Quote: *"Too much ego, too much time in the spotlight make it very difficult for highly talented collection of people to archive phenomenal results."*

Topic: Three Things That Kill Good Visions

1. Ego or the feelings that one can do something better than the other person.
2. Strong desire to take credits for good works instead of looking for good results.
3. Refusal to give others the chances to develop themselves out of fear of losing relevance.

Debate This Issue: Are talented Nigerians motivated to perform better in their careers if they are given credits or money?

Mark Twain's Quote: *"Keep away from people who belittle your ambition. Small people always do that but the really great people make you feel that you too can become great."*

Topic: Three Things That Can Misdirect People

1. Bad influence of other people either through associations or conversations with them.
2. Misinformation through means of education or information like the media or publications.
3. Dirty or immoral things through means of entertainments like music or movies .

Debate This Issue: Are Nigerian youths made more corrupt through music or movies?

Dipo Toby Alakija's Quote: *"A misinformed society is a deformed society just as a misdirected youth is a misguided future."*

Topic: Three Consequences Of Misinformation

1. It makes people ignorant and unproductive .
2. It creates vice rings like cultism and fosters all kinds of vices and crimes in the society.
3. Misinformation, especially through incitements or hate speeches can lead to destructions of lives and properties.

Debate This Issue: Are Nigerian youths easily deceived or not?

Eleanor Roosevelt's Quote: *"No one can make you feel inferior without your consent."*

Topic: Three Things Inferiority Complex Can Do In Your Life

1. It can destroy your potentials or chances to become great.
2. It can force you to surrender your dreams or visions to people who has no chances of becoming great like you.
3. It kills the ability to progress in your visions, creating fear of opinions of others and removing ability to think straight and through.

Debate This Issue: Is it right for parents to influence the careers of their children or not?

Zig Ziglar's Quote: *"The present day is important to you for this reason: you can waste it or use it, but no matter how you spend it, you've traded a day of your life for it."*

Topic: Three Things People Must Do With Their Youthful Days

1. They must enhance their values in life by getting educated or acquiring skills which they would need as they grow into adults.
2. They must encourage other youths in their careers so as that they would not constitute nuisance to them or to the society in future.
3. They must live responsible instead of wayward life because whatever they do now will reflect in their future.

Debate This Issue: Can Government influence how youths will spend their time or not?

Kenneth Copeland's Quote: *"Your gift will take you places but your character will keep you there."*

Topic: Three Things About Attitudes Of Citizens Of Any Nation

1. The progression or regression of the nation in its noble cause largely depends on the patriotic or unpatriotic attitudes of the citizens.
2. Positive attitudes of the citizens are the major things that can bring about positive change in the society.
3. Friendly attitudes attract friendly people while hostile attitudes attract enemies.

Debate This Issue: Is Nigeria a hostile or friendly nation, going by what is observed in the society?

CORRECTING THE DEFECTIVE NATIONAL PSYCHE THROUGH VALUE EDUCATION AND ORIENTATION PROGRAMMES

Seminar Paper For Potential Value Teachers, Resource Persons, Educationists, Leaders And Other Adults

INTRODUCTION

While presenting a paper on how to restore the National Value System of Nigeria to all students in a State Government Secondary Schools at different days, the author of this paper used the story: The Generational Ship in this book to introduce the paper.

There were two responses in both Junior and Senior Secondary Schools which reveal the fact that the more children grow up in a bad system, the more they are hardened. While the mobile phone of the author was stolen in the among Senior Secondary School Students, a Student in Junior School who just completed her Primary School and admitted into Junior Secondary School asked, "Who is going to fix the engine of this ship?" It was a very rewarding question that made up for the stolen mobile phone. Thus students who are considered the 3rd generation are to think of how to fix the engines. The following items were shared with them as ways they need to fix the engines of the boat.

Firstly, they need to understand the reason the belief in God is embedded in the National Anthem and The Pledge To Nigeria, which may be found in the Bible in Proverb 14:34. The passage says that righteousness (right standing with God) exalts (prospers and promotes) a nation but sin (wrong doings) is a reproach (problems or oppressions) to the people. Thus the followings are four ways the National Value System can be reconstructed:

1. Everybody needs to fear and build faith in God of all creations as in the prayers in third stanza of the National Anthem. Research works reveal the fact that God-fearing people are often law-abiding citizens.
2. All Nigerian citizens in old and young Generations who understand the urgent need to reconstruct the dilapidated National Value System must begin to teach others National Values with the use of these resource materials. The Nigerian citizens include Secondary School Students who teach others or debate render speeches on vices, value and virtues in schools, youths who teach others on campuses and in other places, adults who teach their children and other citizens.
3. Literate and patriotic citizens need to seek education for others who are not educated or reorientate or inform those whose perceptions of values are incorrect. The reason the author emphases that a nation that is not informed would be deformed by uninformed members of the society lies in the fact that information is what actually brings about transformation in any given society.
4. Anyone who steals from the nation or anyone through corruption or fraud or make money other illegitimate ways needs to be considered dangerous criminal who is capable of destroying future generations. This is because stealing from especially the nation is a debt which every generation, including unborn children would have to pay with sufferings, pains, hunger and other things that can force them to go into crimes or that can make them destitute.

After explaining the above to the students, according to their levels of understanding, they understood that they also have the responsibilities and moral obligations to repair the main engine of the boat, which is the National Value System by following the National Anthem and fulfilling the pledge they make to Nigeria.

As for the stolen mobile phone in the senior class, through the full cooperation of the Principal and some teachers who all felt concerned, the author was able to identify a prime suspect who is a 18 or 19-year old boy. He was the one who sat beside his laptop bag where the phone was kept while he and his assistance were busy arranging the students and the resource materials.

When the boy was summoned to the Principal's office for questioning, he became so frightened that the suspicions became stronger. The Principal threatened to hand him over to the Police and expel him from school. The author quickly told the Principal to let the boy go on the ground that they did not have enough proof that he actually stole the phone. Of course, the Principal expressed his frustrations, saying that the boy needed to serve as a scape goat. While admitting that he was right, the author told him that his mission in the school was not to catch potential criminals but to transform them into reasonable and responsible citizens. Then he asked the Principal and the teachers who did not seem to understand his point, "even if this boy whose appearance in tattered school uniform that reveals his poor background stole the phone, what makes him different from those who are looting public fund? In fact, as far as the author is concerned, those looting public fund are worse than him because stealing Government money is what makes so many people become criminals. Those who do not want to steal often end up becoming destitutes. Even if adults pretend as if they do not know what is going on in the society, these young ones know exactly what is happening around them. Thus it is obvious that the reason most people are in politics today is not because they want to serve the nation but because they want to loot public treasury."

This and many other experiences reveal the fact that the Nigerian National Psyche is grossly defective. Unless something is done to arrest the situation, the crime rate in the country is going to increase drastically.

Before anyone can correct the national psyche, however, there is need to identify errors that are mostly responsible for the problems in Nigeria.

ERRORS THAT CAUSE THE DEFECTIVE NATIONAL PSYCHE AND THE MESS IN NIGERIA

What Nigeria is presently experiencing now was predicted about 25 years ago in the cause of research works on causes of social vices and crimes in Nigeria. This is when errors in (I) The System Of Education (II) The National Value System and (III) Enforcement of Laws, Rules and Order could have been easily corrected. These errors, especially in the National Value System can no longer be easily rectified through political or economic machineries for the mere fact that the perceptions of values in most aspects of life in Nigeria are incorrect, going by the results of research works. Hence, while delivery CEMS papers during seminar on Value Initiative Programme (VIP) and Student Orientation Studies (SOS) that was held in conjunction with Oyo State Ministry Of Education in 2020, the author revealed that teachers are the last hope of Nigeria. Invariably, the education sector is in the best position to correct these errors; forestalling future vices and crimes by simply inculcating values and spirit of patriotism in the minds of all categories of citizens, especially children and youths who are future parents and leaders of tomorrow. In spite of the sensitive position of this sector, it is faced with lots of challenges and threats to its abilities to function effectively.

HIGHLIGHTS OF CHALLENGES IN THE EDUCATION SECTOR IN NIGERIA

Attempting to find out the challenges in the education sector in each State in Nigeria is like trying to diagnose the ailments of every sick person in the country. Aside from the time and cost of collating data, there are far too many factors that would make it almost impossible to get accurate information. However, about 25-year old research works reveal the commonest problems in the education sector, some of which were examined during the seminar on Value Initiative Programmes (VIP) and Student Orientation Studies (SOS) in Oyo State in 2020.

The following illustrations and observations in primary education in Nigeria are extracted from one of the seminar papers:

"...The primary education which is faced with lots of challenges in Nigeria is the foundation and the most vital aspect of the education system in every nation. To better appreciate this fact, there is need to consider the laying of the foundation of a skyscraper, which needs to go down first before it goes up. The foundation of a skyscraper is always laid on the rocky part of the underground so that when it goes up into the sky, it would not be crumbled by the weight of the entire building. Similarly, for children to build their future or careers in life, their primary education must be of very good quality. If it is very good, they find it easy to continue their academic quests at secondary and tertiary levels. Once they can read, write, communicate effectively in the official language and master the basic principles of Mathematics at primary level, they find it easy to acquire formal or informal education at other levels. For this reason, primary education in every nation is vital and its quality must not be compromised with for any reason. Federal and State Governments, therefore, need to secure quality primary education and make it mandatory for every child in Nigeria.

"It is also observed during the research works that most Nigerian children, particularly those in public schools are not getting quality primary education due to unqualified workers who man the sensitive positions of primary school teachers. These observations and CEMS recommendations were presented to all State Ministries of Education (SMoEs) in Nigeria 2017..."

REBUILDING THE NATION BY REBUILDING THE NATIONAL VALUE SYSTEM

National Values In this context can simply be described as what the nation stands for as the right thing and what it stands against as the wrong thing. Thus National Value System can be explained as the machinery in the form of regulations, rules and order that ensure that citizens are reasonable and responsible enough to always do the right things and sanction anyone who does not do the right thing or who does not fit into the system.

Again, with references to the author's paper, titled: "The Right Values And Quality Education", the followings are ascertained:

"... The Nigerian Value System is getting paralyzed by media, entertainment industries, social, economic, political, academic, religious organizations and institutions which are supposed to reinforce it. All these, particularly the media and entertainment industries have wrecked more havoc on the Nigerian Value System than any other thing.

"... The results of research works also indicate that the Value System is what actually powers or influences the working conditions of other machineries like the economic, social, academic and political machineries. Thus it is possible for academically and politically sound leaders to be unable to lead others in the on the right path if they are unpatriotic or their perceptions of values are incorrect.

"... It is worthy note the following observations in the Nigerian socio-political and other systems, including education sector and Civil Service which make it hard for the nation to make meaningful progress:

1. Political Favouritism Within The Systems: A lot of people who are either not qualified to occupy some sensitive positions in the society or not capable to undertake some capital intensive projects are given appointments or awarded contracts probably because they or their relations are connected with some people in Federal or State Governments. There was a year in Nigeria when one of the candidates for the positions of Ambassadors was told to sing the National Anthem during the interview, which was viewed on television. He could not sing it and yet he was able to pass through the screening of the then members of the House of Assembly. One of the implications of watching on TV a person who cannot sing the National Anthem vying for a leadership position is for viewers, especially youths to conclude that the contents of The Anthem and The Pledge To Nigeria are irrelevant.
2. The System Makes Government To Be Too Involved In Businesses: True capitalism gives the people power to run businesses while the Government is more concerned with administrations. The involvements of Governments in so many businesses in the name of job creations make politics attractive and very lucrative even for jobless touts to get involved. Besides this, Government hardly makes anything called gain out of these businesses. Instead, it gives room for wastage.
3. Employments Of Too Many Staffs In The Civil Service: By getting involved in too many businesses, most of which can be effectively handled by private sectors, so many staffs are engaged in the Civil Service; making the Government expensive to run. Besides that, many unnecessary jobs are created for Government employees who would task the national or state treasury while in service and after they retire. This always poses challenges of paying workers and pensioners. When there are too many salaries to pay, there would be too little to invest in the future of young Nigerians. The author was able to observe this when he was an Admin Personnel at the Federal Civil Service where he voluntarily retired in 1998.

The above and other reasons make both State and Federal Governments unable to meet up to their responsibilities to most citizens. If any Government is unable to meet up to its responsibilities, these are the things to expect:

1. Lack Of Morale And Dedication In The Civil Service: This always lead to poor quality or no services to the citizens, some of which can pose threats to lives.
2. Bribery And Corruption: Although other factors like acts of unfaithfulness, disloyalty and dishonesty contribute a lot to bribery and corruption within the system but one of the major causes is the corrupt Governments that always corrupt the Civil Service and other sectors, especially if they divert public fund to private purses. Some Governments go as far as taking loans outside Nigeria, diverting some of them to private purses.
3. Vices And Crimes Would Increase: This is another serious effect if Governments do not meet up to their responsibilities to the people. Once crimes increase, lives and properties may be so unsecured that people may be forced to take up arms in order to protect themselves or their properties. No matter how much adults are informed on values or how many moral

lessons young ones are taught in schools or at homes, one should expect little or no effect on them if their environments are characterized with sufferings; vices and crimes. Thus it is safe to conclude that Government that is not responsible breeds a society of irresponsible citizens just as rogue parents breeds rogue children. The rogues that were born the day before yesterday are the causes of the vices of yesterday. The ones that are born yesterday are the causes of the vices of today. The ones that are born today are the ones that will cause the vices of tomorrow with the adverse effects on the society. Anyone who denies these facts about the state of the nation may be thinking like a sick man who claims to be healthy instead of seeing a doctor until the sickness either knocks him down or terminates his life.

The purpose of this paper, however, is not to paint a hopeless situation but to identify the challenges in rebuilding Nigeria, through Value Education And Orientation Programmes. The solution, according to the results of research works, lies with all parents who lead their children, teachers who lead their students, political, community and other leaders who lead other citizens on the right paths.

www.ingramcontent.com/pod-product-compliance
Lightning Source LLC
LaVergne TN
LVHW010358160826
845677LV00005BA/1313
9789783624016